VINTAGE ADELAIDE ›

VINTAGE ADELAIDE ›

Beautiful buildings from the Adelaide Square Mile

REVISED EDITION

Peter Fischer / Kay Hannaford Seamark

East Street Publications

Published by
East Street Publications
11 Gibson Street
Bowden, SA 5007, Australia
www.eaststreet.com.au

Copyright © 2005 Peter Fischer and Kay Hannaford Seamark

All rights reserved. Without limiting the rights under copyright above,
no part of this publication shall be reproduced, stored in or introduced
into a retrieval system, or transmitted in any form or by any means
(electronic, mechanical, photocopying, recording or otherwise),
without the prior permission of both the copyright owner
and the publisher of this book.

An earlier black and white edition of this updated book was first published
by Heritage Press in 1989. Copyright © Peter Fischer and Kay Hannaford.

National Library of Australia Cataloguing-in-Publication data:

Fischer, Peter, 1951–.
       Vintage Adelaide

Rev. ed.
Includes index.
ISBN 1 9210 3706 7
1. Historic buildings—South Australia—Adelaide—Pictorial works.
2. Adelaide (S. Aust.)—Buildings, structures, etc.—Pictorial works.
I. Hannaford, Kay. II Title.

720.994231

Produced in South Australia

Book designed by Alexander Bianchini-Kometer of East Street Publications
Printed by Custom Press, 19 East Street, Brompton, SA 5007

Contents

Acknowledgements	01
Introduction	02
Art Gallery of South Australia	04
Austral Hotel	06
Adelaide Club	08
Queen Adelaide Club	10
North Terrace Townhouse	12
Hartley Building	14
Armoury	16
Destitute Asylum Buildings	18
Destitute Asylum Chapel	20
Bethlehem Lutheran Church	22
South Australian Museum East Wing	24
Woodman's Inn	26
Adelaide Arcade	28
Band Rotunda	30
Holy Trinity Church	32
Old Parliament House	34
Parliament House	36
Adelaide Fruit and Produce Exchange	38
Palm House	40
Government House	42
Hampshire Hotel	44

Edmund Wright House	46
Magistrates Court	48
Adelaide Railway Station	50
Botanic Chambers	52
Menz Biscuit Factory	54
Newmarket Hotel	56
West's Coffee Palace	58
Colonial Store	60
Roman Catholic Chapel	62
Ayers House	64
Dimora	66
Mounted Police Barracks	68
Adelaide Town Hall	70
Queen's Chambers	72
Hindley Street Offices	74
Bonython Hall	76
St Francis Xavier Cathedral	78
Mitchell Building	80
North Lodge	82
Adelaide Gaol	84
Albert Bridge	86
Glossary	89
Notes>Architects	91
Index	99

ACKNOWLEDGEMENTS › Our special thanks to

Marianne Treffers and Bob Seamark for their support, advice and encouragement. Keelan Fischer for technical assistance. Ross Anderson, Pat Stretton, Jan Forbes, Kate McDougall and Liz Vines for their special insights and information.
Michaela Andreyev, Jane Macduff and Alex Bianchini-Kometer of East Street Publications for their infectious enthusiasm and total professionalism.

The staff at the State Library of South Australia for their excellent service and assistance.

The authors of all previous research documents and books about Adelaide's heritage for their information and inspiration and, in particular:
The Heritage of The City of Adelaide – An Illustrated Guide produced by the Corporation of the City of Adelaide in 1996.
Sculptors in Space: South Australian Architects 1836-1986, by Michael Page.
The Queen Adelaide Club: A history of the Club to mark the 75th Anniversary, compiled by the History Subcommittee, April 1984.

All the people who cherish and have worked to build, save and restore vintage Adelaide buildings, including the Adelaide City Council and State Government of Environment and Heritage.

INTRODUCTION >

Adelaide has a special place in the hearts of both its residents and visitors, who are often surprised at its charm and accessibility. It is one of the most livable cities in the world and its inhabitants relish Adelaide's Mediterranean climate, its human scale and splendid lifestyle. Visitors appreciate these same advantages: ease of finding their way around, being able to walk to many places of interest and an ambience that is serene, seductive and memorable. It's no coincidence that Adelaide is the perfect venue for festivals, conventions and lively events enthusing visitors and locals alike.

That Adelaide still retains its grace and elegance today would be gratifying to the visionaries who designed and began building this city over a hundred and seventy years ago. Proudly the first Australian colony settled with free (non-convict) immigrants, these Europeans began arriving in 1836 to join the Kaurna Aboriginal people, 'a dignified and gentle people' on their land that became known as the Adelaide Plains. The site chosen for the city nestled between a range of wooded hills to the east, St Vincent's Gulf with its benign coastline and natural harbour to the west and a river providing fresh (for a time) water running through its midst.

The reigning British monarch of the day, King William IV requested that the new city be named in honour of his consort, Queen Adelaide. Colonel William Light, appointed Surveyor General, arrived on the good ship *Rapid* and set about mapping out the capital city in two sections, North and South Adelaide, on either side of the river. The result is arguably one of the best-planned cities in the world, a military grid of major and minor streets encased in tree-lined terraces surrounded on all sides by spacious parklands, the width of a cannon shot. The city or business centre (formerly South Adelaide) is bounded by four main terraces—North, South, East and West—measuring roughly a square mile with a town square as focal point in the middle and smaller greens or squares in the centre of each quarter.

The first buildings abutted the river for ease of access to water and so North Terrace became home to the city's earliest and most important buildings. First there were tents and as stone was quarried nearby or arrived as ships' ballast, churches, inns, shops, a gaol, a train station and modest houses, including the Governor's residence on the corner of King William Street were gradually built. The houses of parliament were erected nearby and moving east along North Terrace, the cultural precincts and centres of learning took their places along with a hospital adjoining the Botanic Gardens at the East Terrace corner.

City buildings spread south as roads and services were established. Victoria Square, named after the new British monarch, took its rightful place as the town centre flanked by the imposing Municipal Buildings, General Post Office, Treasury, Government Offices, Catholic Cathedral and Law Courts. The Central Produce Market opened nearby in 1869 and still flourishes today.

By the 1880s, when the fledgling colony's fortunes had stabilised, humble single-storey pubs made way for grand corner hotels and thatched cottages were replaced with imposing bluestone mansions along the terraces. By this time, substantial villas, hotels, offices, stores, churches, factories and brick and stone workers' cottages lined the major and minor streets within.

It's ironic that Colonel Light's military approach to town planning is the very thing that gives Adelaide its serenity and peace. Traffic flows easily on the wide streets, the squares provide breathing spaces amidst a bustling city and the parklands act as a hallowed buffer from the now sprawling suburbs.

We are fortunate that Adelaide has retained many of its earliest buildings, designed and erected with such optimism and pride. They are now treasured for the very special character they bequeath to this city and its people.

The buildings in this book are a diverse collection of some of the city's finest, chosen on our interpretation of visual, historical and architectural interest.

The images were produced using a digital enhancement technique. A series of photographs was taken of each building and transferred to a computer. These images were combined and processed to isolate and enhance each building within its environment and to highlight its key features.

We hope you enjoy the richness and diversity of Adelaide's built heritage as much as we do. For as long as it is prized and preserved, we are all the beneficiaries.

ART GALLERY OF SOUTH AUSTRALIA › North Terrace

South Australia's art collection was originally housed, along with the State Library and Museum collections, in the 1860 Institute building on the corner of North Terrace and Kintore Avenue. As these collections outgrew this space, specific buildings were erected for each, further along North Terrace.

The art collection was the last to have its own home and the Art Gallery building in Classical Revival style was opened in April, 1899. It had a small Palladian style portico with an arched entrance, a stone and iron fence and a gate opening onto North Terrace.

Alexander Melrose, a member of the Art Gallery Board, gave £10 000 in 1934 in memory of his parents; his father, George Melrose, was a pioneer in the pastoral industry. This bequest, supplemented by government funds, enabled the gallery to be extended. He also sponsored the Melrose Prize for portrait painting, first awarded in 1929. Winners have included well-known Australian artists Ivor Hele, Russell Drysdale and Jacqueline Hick.

The addition of the Melrose Wing and the present much larger vestibule with classically detailed facade was completed in 1936.

The massive stone columns were turned on site by a large improvised lathe driven by an eight cylinder motor borrowed from a Ford truck. A forty-four gallon drum held the water needed to increase the capacity of the cooling system and jarrah wedges were used as the cutting tools, wearing away the stone as the engine chugged on.

A three-storey wing at the rear of the building was added in 1962 to accommodate more gallery space and offices and extensive alterations to the older sections were needed in the late 1970s to bring the gallery up to international exhibition standards. The impressive West Wing extensions which opened in March 1996, have doubled the size of the Gallery.

The Art Gallery of South Australia today houses wonderful collections of Australian, European and Asian art with generous private donations providing almost ninety per cent of the collection.

AUSTRAL HOTEL 〉 205 Rundle Street

The Austral Hotel is the easternmost section of an unusually large complex including fourteen shops, built for the South Australia Company in the 1880s. The westernmost end has traditionally been occupied by Malcolm Reid and Co., merchants of Adelaide whose business expanded to include branches in Broken Hill, Johannesburg and London.

The architect was William McMinn and construction proceeded from east to west, with the three-storey eastern end of the building opened in 1880 as the Family Hotel. Work continued until all the shops were completed in 1883. The whole complex boasts an Italianate influence and is built of squared sandstone with stucco string-courses and window surrounds. The hotel name was changed three times in as many years, until it was named the Austral in 1898.

Adelaide has retained many of its interesting corner hotels from the 1880s period but this one is particularly significant for its chamfered corner—bevelled off equally on both sides—and tiered balcony of cast-iron lace, a later addition. A central pediment has been removed and leadlight glass added to the ground floor verandah.

The Austral Hotel has added its own vibrancy to the revival of the east end of Rundle Street as a centre for eating and entertainment since the 1980s. The hotel used to advertise with the slogan 'See you down the Nostril' and many people still call it the 'Nostril' today.

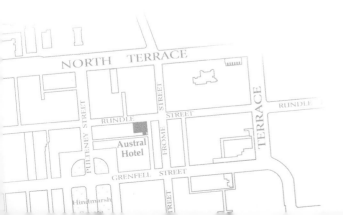

ADELAIDE CLUB > 165 North Terrace

When the imposing Adelaide Club was first erected in 1863–64 directly opposite Government House on North Terrace, its grandeur was emphasized by the fact that, until 1870, it abutted a humble thatched cottage, one of several known as Irish Row.

Gentlemen's clubs were common in cities of the British Empire. The first South Australian Club, designed by George Strickland Kingston, was located in Wakefield Street but was short lived, closing in 1843. The establishment of the Adelaide Club was sponsored by a group of businessmen and farmers who had profited during the colony's early years of rapid growth, propelling themselves into the role of South Australian gentry. Many of the Adelaide Club's founders and members were also the colony's leaders of commerce, industry and politics and it was often joked that more of the decisions affecting the development of South Australia were made in the Adelaide Club than diagonally opposite in Parliament House. Of course, many of their members were one and the same.

Designed by Edward Angus Hamilton and built of Dry Creek stone with brick dressings and exquisite apricot marble on the front steps, the Adelaide Club shows classic balance with the windows slightly decreasing in size with each storey. Its cantilevered balcony originally extended right across the building's facade. One can easily imagine the gentlemen members strolling out onto the balcony after dinner, cigar and a port in hand, to peer over the walls of Government House or even admire the statuary in Prince Henry Gardens opposite. When the replica of Canova's partially clad *Venus* was unveiled in the early 1900s it is rumoured that members of the Adelaide Club had her moved from behind a tree so that they could admire her from the balcony.

One outstanding example of the influence of members of the Adelaide Club was the idea to establish a Festival of Arts for Adelaide. This had its genesis in the dining room of the Adelaide Club in the 1950s and since the first biennial Adelaide Festival was staged in 1960, it has had a profound impact on the cultural life and economic development of South Australia.

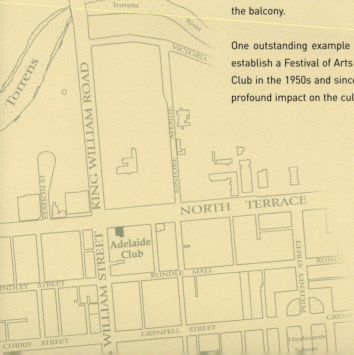

QUEEN ADELAIDE CLUB › 182–184 North Terrace

Some forty-five years after the formation of the Adelaide Club for gentlemen, its female equivalent, the Queen Adelaide Club, was established in the next block along North Terrace.

Originally built as doctors' rooms, the corner building of the three adjoining buildings now occupied by the Queen Adelaide Club on the corner of Stephens Place was built in 1895 for Dr Thomas Cawley. He founded the South Australian branch of the Australian Medical Association. Additions were made in 1897 and 1900 and a verandah on this building was removed by 1908 to allow more light into the downstairs rooms, leaving the cantilevered balcony intact.

At a meeting held in a private sitting room in 1909, the wives of many of Adelaide's leading businessmen discussed the formation of a ladies club similar to clubs becoming popular in London. Addressing the meeting was Mrs George Box, a widow from Melbourne who had moved to Adelaide with her young daughter and was seeking a career. Her Adelaide solicitor suggested that she consider starting a ladies club and the assembled group agreed to a club that was 'residential, social and non-political'. Each member of the provisional committee submitted a list of names of women whom they considered suitable for membership and the club began with 300 members. Mrs Box, described as not only competent but 'elegant', became the first manager and secretary of the Queen Adelaide Club and was referred to as the Proprietor.

The residential aspect of the club was particularly important, since women visiting Adelaide could not stay alone in hotels in those days and the only alternative accommodation was boarding houses.

Two club by-laws passed in the early years are of interest. One, that no hospital nurses be permitted in the club except in grave emergencies, attests to the members' desire that the club not become a de facto hospital. The other, that no cats or dogs or other animals be admitted to the club, came into being after a British visitor smuggled a kangaroo rat into her room, with quite a deal of resultant damage.

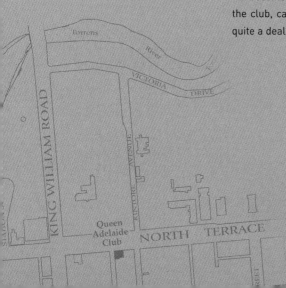

NORTH TERRACE TOWNHOUSE ❯ 261 North Terrace

This elegant townhouse near the eastern end of North Terrace is one of the few examples of a private residence surviving from the 1880s, when North Terrace was lined with fashionable two-storey homes, mainly occupied by the medical fraternity and lawyers. Many of these mansions were built as homes, some as professional rooms and some a combination of both. This building occupies the site of two former dwellings.

Another exceptional example of a William McMinn design, it is built of finely dressed, square-cut sandstone and distinguished by ground floor Ionic columns and an imported slate mansard roof, including a widow's walk and an elaborate attic window.

The house was built between 1881 and 1883 for Arthur Waterhouse, a financier and developer, who never actually lived there. It was initially leased for three years to Sir William Milne, President of the Legislative Council, who lived with his family at 'Sunnyside', a mansion in the foothills at Beaumont. He probably used the house while in town on business. The townhouse went on to be leased by a series of professional men including Walter Bagot, a partner in the architectural firm Woods Bagot.

For much of the twentieth century, the building was used as medical or professional rooms. However the house has now been reconverted to an elegant private residence. During the renovations an ungainly besser block front-addition was removed, restoring the façade to the original and beautiful design. The current proud owners are Raymond and Rosemary Michell.

HARTLEY BUILDING › University of Adelaide, Kintore Avenue

Built around 1925 in the Spanish Mission style, the Hartley Building is a distinctive landmark in Kintore Avenue and an unusual design for an Adelaide institution. It was designed by George Gavin Lawson, a Scot who had worked in South Africa and when the competition for the design of the Australian Federal Capital (later Canberra) was advertised internationally in 1911, he applied albeit unsuccessfully. However his interest in Australia had been aroused and he moved to Queensland the following year and to South Australia in the early 1920s. His work with the Government Architect in Chief involved several institutions and he took deliberate departures from 'institutional styles' to make his buildings more friendly for their users.

The Hartley Building is named after John Anderson Hartley, a prominent figure in education circles in the late nineteenth century. He came to South Australia to become the second headmaster of Prince Alfred College and went on to become Inspector-General of Schools and head of the State Education System. He was tragically killed in 1896 when he collided with a horse while riding his newly acquired bicycle.

This building was the first in Adelaide to be purpose-built for teacher training. It is now used as the Elder School of Music under the auspices of the University of Adelaide.

Spanish Mission style features of the Hartley Building include a terracotta tiled roof, semi-circular windows in the towers, wide eaves, shady verandahs with sturdy double columns and simple, restrained cast-iron railings.

The design reflects attempts at the time to move away from imported English and central European forms and develop more suitable warm-climate styles of architecture to express an Australian vernacular.

ARMOURY › North Terrace
Behind South Australian Museum

Built of limestone with brick dressings, the southern section of the Mounted Police Barracks complex behind the South Australian Museum became known as the Armoury. The architect, William Bennett Hays, designed Old Parliament House on North Terrace of the same materials in the same year. The east and west wings of the Armoury were built in the style of bachelors' residences and were occupied by inspectors. Although built for the Police Force, the Armoury and inspectors' residences became associated with military history and it was from here that the South Australian troops left for the Boer War in South Africa.

Originally a single-storey building, extensions to the Armoury occurred in 1858, including a second floor and an exterior double-flight of stone steps to an upper floor. From 1857 to 1870, this was the headquarters for the Australian Imperial Forces while they were stationed in South Australia. Each Sunday morning they provided a colourful spectacle, marching down North Terrace to attend the service at Holy Trinity Church.

DESTITUTE ASYLUM BUILDINGS › off Kintore Avenue

Behind the State Library of South Australia

Although Adelaide's origins were convict-free, the colony did not escape poverty and misery, as the buildings of the Destitute Asylum attest. This was a large government institution erected to care for the poor and infirm and was based on the Dickensian model of workhouses in England.

Work on the Destitute Asylum began in the 1850s, probably under the supervision of government architect William Bennett Hays and continued over the next thirty years. The complex originally comprised a large number of buildings grouped around a series of quadrangles. Four buildings still remain. Included was a female immigration depot, where young immigrant women, deserted wives and children could stay until placed; the forerunner of later migrant hostels. In 1863 the compound became an asylum for all destitute people, with schoolrooms, dormitories, stores, hospital facilities and laundries.

The two-storey bluestone Lying-in Hospital (shown here) built in 1877 for 'pregnant and diseased women' was the most important building in the complex. Many of its early inmates were young Irish girls, escaping the potato famine in Ireland in 1846-50. They were shipped out to the colonies by the thousands to work as domestic servants. However they were unskilled and unable to find work and many resorted to prostitution.

One of the small remaining buildings across the quadrangle was the Labour Ward. The Lying-in Hospital was used until 1918 and is now part of the Migration Museum which exists, appropriately, to focus attention on the diverse groups of people from all over the world who, for equally diverse reasons, have made South Australia their home.

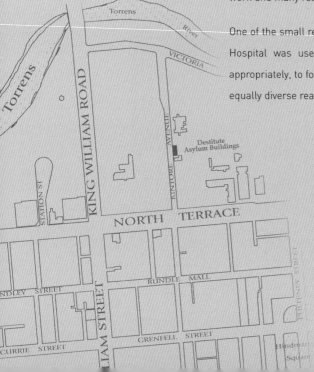

DESTITUTE ASYLUM CHAPEL ❯ off Kintore Avenue
Behind the State Library of South Australia.

The stone chapel, one of the complex of Destitute Asylum buildings, was originally built in 1867 as a schoolroom for the children of the soldiers stationed in the nearby barracks. The schoolroom was also associated with a girls' reformatory near this site. At times the unruly girls could be heard yelling abuse as far away as Rundle Street and they showed scant regard for government property.

In a move which seems shocking today, a cell block was added to the schoolroom in 1872 and the girls were threatened with incarceration if they misbehaved. It is unlikely that the girls were actually locked up but the heavy stone wall at the end of the chapel facing Kintore Avenue, was originally iced with broken glass to prevent escape and still conceals three tiny cells.

Later in the 1870s the schoolroom became the chapel for the Destitute Asylum. The building has been converted to a café for some years.

BETHLEHEM LUTHERAN CHURCH > 170 Flinders Street

The spire of the Bethlehem Lutheran Church would look more at home in Bavaria or even in the Barossa Valley than in the central business district of Adelaide.

The Lutheran Church in Australia began in Adelaide with the arrival in 1839 of the first German immigrants led by Pastor Kavel. Many of these people, fleeing religious persecution in the Prussian Union, settled in Hahndorf in the Adelaide Hills or in the Barossa Valley. These early Lutherans arrived belonging to one church but split over a doctrinal question into the Evangelical Lutheran Church in Australia and United Evangelical Lutheran Church of Australia. These denominations later rejoined to form the Lutheran Church of Australia in 1966.

This church was established for the city congregation of Evangelical Lutherans, separate from the United Evangelical Lutherans who worshipped at St Stephen's Church in Wakefield Street.

Built in 1872, the church is bluestone with rendered detailing and designed in early Gothic style by James Cumming. The stucco on the tower and quoins is lined to resemble stone. The tower has a large chamber, designed for three bells that were cast from a cannon captured from the French (during the Franco-Prussian War 1870) and presented to the church by Prince Bismarck on behalf of the Kaiser; however, they never arrived in South Australia as the vessel carrying the bells was lost.

The church remains in remarkably original condition and still seats between four and five hundred worshippers. A classic style German 2000 pipe organ, the first of its kind in Adelaide, takes up the full width of the gallery. Vestries were added in 1961.

SOUTH AUSTRALIAN MUSEUM EAST WING > North Terrace

Many of Adelaide's grandest buildings were built in stages, years apart and the South Australian Museum is no exception. This 1915 section of the South Australian Museum was the third stage of a plan for one large complex, housing the Museum and the State Library next door.

A close look at the Museum from North Terrace reveals the similarity of this wing with the Mortlock Library building to the west, although the latter was built thirty years earlier. The red brick section known as the Museum's North Wing linking the Library and Museum was built in 1895 and intended as a temporary structure, to be replaced with a much more imposing stone edifice but this never eventuated.

Both the Mortlock Library and the Museum East Wing are French Renaissance style, with finely detailed stonework, a mansard roof, dormer windows and an octagonal tower. The Museum wing took seven years to build because of the difficulty of finding sufficient stone and it has only one tower, contrasting with its neighbour's two.

The South Australian Museum's natural history collection is most famous for its Australian Aboriginal and Pacific collections and the treasures in its Ancient Egyptian room. Other rare items can be seen outside the building. A fossil tree trunk near the main entrance is thought to be from a species of eucalyptus dating back more than two million years. A three thousand-year-old Egyptian column, from a temple built by Rameses II on the upper Nile, is the oldest non-aboriginal artifact in Australia. It is now housed just inside the glass entrance in front of the North wing, where it is protected from the elements.

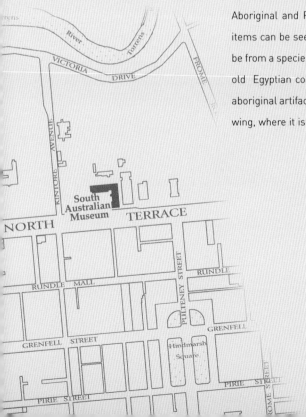

WOODMAN'S INN > 233–237 Grenfell Street

The original hotel built on this site in 1839, called simply The Woodman, was a popular refreshment stop for the tiersmen, or woodmen, bringing timber from the Tiers (the Adelaide Hills) to the timber yard on the site of the Botanic Hotel two blocks to the north. The Woodman changed its name to the Electric Light Hotel in 1901, when the Electric Lighting and Traction Company had built its power station almost next door on Grenfell Street.

The early building was then demolished to make way for the present hotel, built in 1906 as the Producers Hotel by the South Australian Brewing Company, to take advantage of the trade generated by Charlick's New Market across the road. It became known as the Woodman's Inn in the 1980s. While the markets opposite were in operation, the hotel was always open very early in the mornings, sometimes all night and served hearty breakfasts at the front bar for market workers.

The Queen Anne style architecture, with its distinctive tiled roof, is unusual in Adelaide and the upper-storey facade is an excellent example of the design work of this period. Its distinctive style complements the old power station building, now the Tandanya Aboriginal Cultural Centre next door and of course, the flamboyant Edwardian style Fruit and Produce Exchange facades opposite.

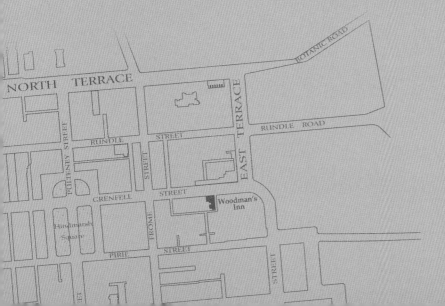

ADELAIDE ARCADE › Rundle Mall

The completion of the elegant Adelaide Arcade in 1885 heralded the transformation of Rundle Street into Adelaide's premier retail precinct. These were boom years; the colony was flourishing and the scale, materials and styles of buildings erected during the 1880s reflected this optimism. Adelaide Arcade with its adjoining Gay's Arcade (named after Patrick Gay, one of the original shareholders) opening onto Twin Street, were fine examples of Victorian shopping arcades.

Originally designed with fifty shops, each with its own internal staircase leading to a workroom above, Adelaide Arcade featured Carrara marble flooring with black and white tile designs, three fountains, tearooms in the basement and Turkish baths in one corner. The building of brick, cast iron and plate glass, cost £30 000 and took only five months to complete, which was a record in the colony at that time. Designed by James Cumming, it was one of the first buildings in Adelaide to use electric lighting, although gas lamps were also fitted to each shop.

In 1968 the building was extensively altered to increase the size and number of shops. A walkway was added at first floor level and most of the internal staircases disappeared. In 1980 a fire completely gutted Gay's Arcade and severely damaged Adelaide Arcade to the tune of A$2 million.

An octagonal tower and dome featuring an early version of the Australian Coat of Arms adds to the skyscape at each end of the building which runs the length of the block between Rundle Mall and Grenfell Street. The Adelaide Arcade was built twenty-four years before an Australian Coat of Arms was officially proclaimed in 1908. Competitions had been conducted throughout the land and the Adelaide Arcade's promoters took a punt by adopting the design they thought would win. The final design for the Australian Coat of Arms does feature a kangaroo and an emu (seen here in the picture); however they are on opposite sides to the Adelaide Arcade's speculative version.

Since the early 1900s when a caretaker died in the building (his head caught in the electricity generator), sporadic reports of inexplicable phenomena have led to the belief that Adelaide Arcade also harbours a resident ghost!

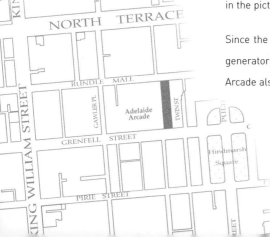

BAND ROTUNDA ❯ Elder Park, off King William Road

Elder Park, on the northern bank of the Torrens Lake, was originally part of the Governor's garden; it was never intended that King William Street should be extended through the garden to North Adelaide.

In 1881, in celebration of the damming of the Torrens River, wealthy landowner and industrialist Sir Thomas Elder offered to donate a bandstand to the city. He also offered to pay £100 towards the erection of the bandstand. The Adelaide City Council deliberated, chose the site for the bandstand and the Government kindly handed over the land.

The bandstand, chosen from a Scottish catalogue, was shipped out from McFarlane's Saracen Foundry in Glasgow and erected in August 1882. More than seven metres in diameter, the octagonal bandstand was a magnificent structure with its canopied roof, domed cupola and cast-iron railings. The land had to be built up some five-and-a-half metres with tons of soil so that the bandstand could be properly admired from King William Road.

The official opening, by Mayor Edwin Smith in November that year, was attended by two thousand people. A special *Rotunda March* was composed for the occasion and played by the Military Band. For some years, the rotunda was the venue for regular performances and open-air concerts on Saturday nights.

The Band Rotunda, one of Adelaide's most delicately styled landmarks, was restored and repainted in its original colours in 1986 to celebrate the State's 150th birthday and its image has been used extensively in tourism marketing as a symbol of Adelaide's grace and elegance.

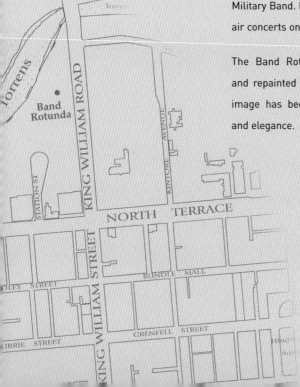

HOLY TRINITY CHURCH › North Terrace

The oldest standing church in the city, Holy Trinity was built within eighteen months of Proclamation Day in 1836 and saw the christenings, marriages and burials of many early South Australians. The first service, the christening of six babies, took place in July 1838, while workmen were still hammering on the last of the roof tiles.

The north-western section of the city was home to all the new arrivals after disembarking from their long sea voyages. Many pitched tents or stayed at Immigration Square, near the corner of West and North Terraces, while they built their own makeshift homes along North Terrace or Hindley Street. Hotels, churches and shops were the next priorities. The Anglicans, affronted by the prefabricated church that had been sent out, commissioned Henry Moseley to build this Victorian Gothic church. However Moseley did such a bad job that it had to be rebuilt later in its present form by Edward Woods.

Trinity Church, as it was originally known, was built of the same stone as Old Parliament House further along North Terrace. The foundation stone was laid by Governor Hindmarsh. The church quickly became too small for the rapidly expanding congregation and within five months, a transept and vestry were added. Five years later the church was pronounced unsafe due to shoddy workmanship and was closed, partly rebuilt and enlarged again. The original tall steeple which had been sent out from England was replaced with an odd-looking belfry that did not seem to match. The church clock, made by the clockmaker to King William IV, became Adelaide's first town clock.

With the arrival of Bishop Short, the colony's first Anglican Bishop, Trinity Church became the procathedral and in July 1848, was consecrated as the Cathedral Church of Holy Trinity. Ten years later, when Christ Church was built in North Adelaide, it became the procathedral until St Peter's Cathedral was eventually built in 1869.

Holy Trinity Church underwent major reconstruction in 1888 and '89, when the walls were raised four to five feet (1.5 metres); the chancel was entirely rebuilt and the tower raised, to the design of Edward Woods. As with Old Parliament House, it was impossible to match the original stone and these additions are still obvious to this day.

The prayer book and Bible used on the voyage out on the HMS *Buffalo* by Charles Beaumont Howard, the first colonial Chaplain, are preserved in the church.

OLD PARLIAMENT HOUSE › North Terrace

This distinctive old stone building opening onto North Terrace on the western side of Parliament House is one of Adelaide's jewels. Before the first Legislative Council chamber was built on this site in the early 1840s, meetings of the Legislative Council were held in the sitting room at Government House.

Designed by William Bennett Hays and built around the original Legislative Council chamber in 1855, Old Parliament House is an outstanding example of early Adelaide architecture. The textured white limestone was quarried from the rear of the site near the present Festival Centre car park and the old Adelaide bricks have been shaped to form intricate designs as quoins, door and window-dressings and parapet.

The building was extended in 1875 to accommodate a growing parliamentary contingent and these additions are obvious by the different colour of the stone. Still more space was needed and in 1889 the House of Assembly moved into the new Parliament House next door. When the Legislative Council followed suit in 1939, Old Parliament House was listed for demolition. Only the outbreak of the Second World War provided enough of a distraction to save the building and its interim uses have included a gymnasium, a social club for railway workers and Government offices.

A wall of the original 1840s chamber was discovered when the present Old Parliament House was renovated in the 1970s. The old wall can be seen inside Old Parliament House today, preserved for posterity. In 1980 it opened as Australia's first museum of constitutional history with electronic wizardry, very avant-garde for its time, guiding visitors through chambers re-enacting the state's political history. Other topical exhibitions and function facilities add to its attraction for both locals and visitors to Adelaide.

PARLIAMENT HOUSE › North Terrace

Adelaide's Parliament House, though considered one of the most awkwardly sited of all Australian State parliament buildings, is one of the grandest buildings in Adelaide. Although arguments raged for and against building it in Victoria Square near the government offices, it occupies a prominent corner of North Terrace and King William Street.

Built in two distinct sections, the only external signs that the western end of the building was constructed fifty years earlier than the central and eastern sections are the lamps on the staircase and six faces carved in the keystones of the upstairs windows. This first section was completed in 1889; the faces are those of leading parliamentarians and Governors of that era. The interiors of each end of the building are stark reflections of the vastly different styles of the Victorian and the art deco eras.

Parliament House was linked originally to the sandstone Legislative Council building (now Old Parliament House) next door by a walkway through a first floor window. The House of Assembly, or Lower House, sat in the new building, while the Legislative Council or Upper House remained in the old building.

In 1936, wealthy Adelaide businessman and philanthropist, Sir Langdon Bonython, gave £100,000 towards the completion of Parliament House to celebrate the State's centenary. Three years later, members of the Legislative Council moved into their austere new chamber, in stark contrast to the ornate high-Victorian House of Assembly chamber with its elaborate coffered ceilings and elegant gasoliers.

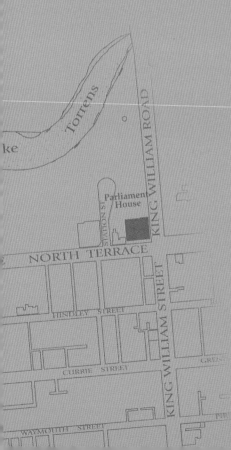

While the whole building was designed by Edmund Wright and Melbourne architect Lloyd Taylor, the plans were altered by Edward Woods who supervised the building of the earlier section. The original design included an enormous central dome and other external embellishments but like the carved faces in the windows, these luxuries had to be foregone on the 1930s addition which completed the building. Parliament House is built of marble from Kapunda, near the Barossa Valley and sits on a base of granite from West Island, off Victor Harbor.

Parliament House has been the setting for much progressive social legislation, including granting women the right to vote in 1894. The South Australian Parliament was the first in Australia to do so and in the same year, was the first place in the world to pass legislation allowing women to sit in Parliament.

ADELAIDE FRUIT AND PRODUCE EXCHANGE ›
Corner East Terrace & Grenfell Street

The history of Adelaide's markets is fascinating. The earliest markets selling garden produce were located at the corner of Rundle Street and Gawler Place in 1840. The first East End Market was established along East Terrace between North Terrace and Rundle Street. Following the example of a grocer named Richard Vaughan, who had sold produce from a trestle in the yard of the Stag Hotel in the early 1860s, other growers and hawkers had congregated there to sell their produce but there was no shelter and they blocked the streets. The City Corporation banned this activity and established its own City Market in 1869, in the block between Gouger and Grote Streets west of Victoria Square. (After a difficult start, it still thrives today as the Adelaide Central Market, a deliciously colourful place to shop for fresh food direct from the growers). But in those early days the City Market had no covered selling areas and as most of the growers were located on the eastern side of the city, they refused to patronise the new site. In 1871 Richard Vaughan purchased the land between North Terrace and Rundle Street, roofed the area and through a Private Member's Bill proclaiming an Act of Parliament, the East End Market became the only market allowed to operate.

In 1903 William Charlick, proprietor of Charlick Brothers, a large fruit, potato and grocery business, offered the land on the corner of East Terrace and Grenfell Street to the East End Market Company, which was looking to expand. When his offer was refused, he decided to build his own market in competition with the East End Market.

The Adelaide Fruit and Produce Exchange which provided complete cover was popularly known then as the New Market and was designed by Henry James Cowell and built in 1904. It operated as a wholesale fruit and vegetable market, selling to the retailers in the early hours of each weekday morning. During the 1930s and 1940s there was a great influx of wholesalers into the markets and in 1943, the South Australian Chamber of Fruit and Vegetable Industries was formed. In 1988, the wholesale markets moved out to Adelaide's northern outskirts and a residential development took their place, rising from behind this extravagant façade.

The Fruit and Produce Exchange building is remarkable for its red brick frontages with rococo cement dressings, classical egg-and-dart moulding, Biblical quotes. 'The earth is the Lord's and the fulness (sic) thereof', and full-blown urns of fruit and vegetables decorating the parapets. The detailing of the embellishments is very fine, especially considering much of it was done in situ. Cowell's row of seven two-storey buildings, one room deep, with ground floor shops and offices or accommodation above, have been retained along with their elaborate timber and cast-iron window mullions on the ground floor.

We can be grateful that these ebullient facades remain as a reminder of the early morning colour, bustling vibrancy and delicious aromas that greeted city workers on market days.

PALM HOUSE ❯ Botanic Gardens, off North Terrace

Lady Musgrave, wife of the South Australian Governor, described the Palm House as a 'fairy palace' when she officially opened this exquisite addition to the Botanic Gardens in 1877.

Dr Richard Schomburgk, the second Director of the Botanic Gardens, is credited with many of the features which still attract thousands of visitors regularly to the gardens, including the Palm House.

The Palm House has a typically Victorian appearance, yet it is Adelaide's first 'modern' building, constructed of iron and glass. The hanging glass technique is still used in buildings today. It was designed by Gustav Runge and shipped in packages from Bremen in West Germany, costing £1087 and weighing 48 000 pounds (21 770 kg). However, by the time the shipment arrived, one third of the 3808 panes of glass had broken and had to be replaced.

Occupying a prime position in the Botanic Gardens, the Palm House was erected on a masonry plinth. Mud from a nearby pond was used to build up a terrace, six feet (1.8 metres) high and thirty feet (9.1 metres) broad on all sides. Dr Schomburgk was responsible for the interior layout and design, which revolves around a central octagonal rotunda supported by Italianate brackets and columns, linked to the north and south entrances by avenues paved with red, black and yellow tiles. The glass is mostly transparent or frosted, with deep rich-blue panes on the borders.

By 1986 the Palm House needed restoration due to corrosion of the iron glazing bars. Restoration work began in 1992 which involved numbering, restoring and reassembling each pillar and pane. On completion it was decided to install a plant display that needed dry and warm conditions to avoid future corrosion. The Gondwanaland exhibit was chosen as Australia and Madagascar were once joined (150 million years ago) and many of Australia's native plants have their origins from that time and are linked to the flora of Madagascar. The cactus garden surrounding the building was also replaced with the original design of sweeping lawns and a gracious balustrade and steps leading to the entrance.

Today the Palm House is the only example of its kind in the world and both it and the unusual plant display draw a great number of visitors.

GOVERNMENT HOUSE › North Terrace

Adelaide's first Governor's residence, built for Governor Hindmarsh, was a humble three-roomed wattle and daub cottage with a calico ceiling, built by the river near the site of the present Railway Station. Government Hut, as it was known, was built by marines from the HMS *Buffalo* and it burnt down within a few years but not before the colony's second incumbent, Governor Gawler, had commissioned the building of a much grander vice-regal residence. This, along with the Adelaide Gaol, bankrupted the colony by 1841 and Governor Gawler was swiftly recalled to England.

The first section of the present Government House, the two-storey Regency style wing facing east, was begun as early as 1839, when most colonists were still living in tents or cottages thatched with reeds from the River Torrens. The architect was George Strickland Kingston and the cost on completion was £5000, more than a year's revenue for the fledgling colony. After Governor Gawler was recalled, a colourful array of Governors followed in his wake, among them Lord Tennyson, son of the famous poet, Sir Mark Oliphant, world-renowned physicist and Dame Roma Mitchell, Australia's first female Supreme Court judge.

The central section of Government House, designed by Edward Hamilton, was added in 1855, during Sir Richard and Lady McDonnell's stay, when the fortunes of the colony were more stable. Constructed of local stone in the Italianate style, it was stuccoed to blend with the Regency section and comprises entrance portico, state dining room, Adelaide room, the Governor's study, a ballroom and the south hall. The west wing, including a billiard room and private secretary's office, completed the building in 1878, during Governor Jervois' term of office.

Colonial women kept a close interest in the Royal Family, as evidenced by a Mrs Allen, in domestic service at Government House during Sir James Ferguson's term (1869-1873). She wrote:

> The fashion of the time was for ladies to limp in their walk as if lame ... the Princess of Wales had a sore foot and, consequently, it was considered the right thing to walk in a halting manner, in fact some went to the length of having one heel of their shoes made shorter than the other.

This Princess of Wales was Princess Alexandra of Denmark who later became Queen consort of King Edward VII.

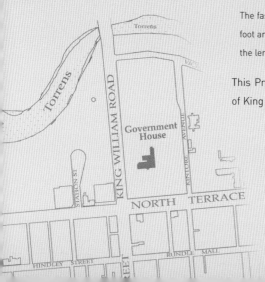

HAMPSHIRE HOTEL › 110 Grote Street

This is one of Adelaide's more diminutive hotels, constructed of brick rather than stone and built in 1911 on the site of an earlier hotel of the same name. The Hampshire Hotel is one of prominent local architect Kenneth Milne's earliest Adelaide buildings; he began practising architecture in Adelaide 1909 after three exciting years developing his ideas in Sydney. The famous scoreboard at the Adelaide Oval is another example of his work at this time.

Milne's buildings reflect elements of the Art Nouveau style and the Hampshire Hotel is a distinctive example. Its features include leadlight windows, typical of their time but unusual in a commercial building; its asymmetry, unusual joinery design under the eaves, cantilevered balcony and timber verandah decoration give it its distinctive style.

This hotel was built for Messrs Chambers and Blades of the Dragon Brewery. The Dragon Brewery was established in the early 1870s, next door to the Green Dragon Hotel on South Terrace. The brewery closed in 1901 but Chambers and Blades continued to supply their many hotels from the Walkerville Cooperative Brewing Company.

EDMUND WRIGHT HOUSE ❯ 59 King William Street

Edmund Wright House, named after its designer Edmund William Wright, is one of Adelaide's most precious assets, cherished for its splendid presence and architectural merit. It is also historically important for its association with the development of financial institutions in Adelaide. Inscribed in gold letters above an inside door in the entrance hall are the words 'After transacting business in a tent, the first building of the Bank of South Australia was opened on North Terrace in 1837'. By 1866, after the mining boom, competition among the banks was fierce and the Bank of South Australia Board purchased the land on which this building now stands, for £10 000. It was twelve years before the building was completed.

A combination of bad management, increased competition and a decision to enter the Melbourne market, all led to the Bank of South Australia's decline. In 1892, the Union Bank took over the business and the Bank of South Australia was formally dissolved on the last day of 1899. This Union Bank building later became the ANZ bank before being threatened with demolition to make way for a twenty-storey office block in 1971. After a protracted public battle during which protestors gathered 58 500 signatures and presented them to Premier Don Dunstan, the government purchased the building and put it to use as government offices. Edmund Wright House became the Registry of Births, Deaths and Marriages and a splendid setting for civil wedding ceremonies. It later housed the History Trust offices and is currently used as the Migrant Resource Centre of South Australia.

Edmund Wright House is one of the most exquisite buildings in the city. Designed in Wright's favourite French Renaissance style, the basic building cost £30 000 but that doubled with the elaborate fixtures, fittings and materials used, many of which were brought from the United Kingdom. Every stone was hand-worked; the exterior stone carving is the work of Scottish sculptor, William J Maxwell who came to South Australia especially to carve the capitals, keystone heads and friezes. The exterior is remarkable for its proportion and detail and the interior is grander still. Carved, highly polished Italian marble columns and a richly decorated ceiling in the entrance hall lead to the old banking chamber, which has an ornate coffered ceiling, original etched glass in the windows and finely carved woodwork.

The South Australian Register of 1 January 1877 reported 'If there is a fault in this magnificent building, it is that of excessive ornamentation'.

MAGISTRATES COURT › Victoria Square

The earliest court hearings were conducted on the HMS *Buffalo*, the ship which carried the first Governor and Supreme Court judge, Justice Jeffcott, to South Australia in December 1836. While this State proudly lays claim to a non-convict settlement, that is not to say that crime and criminals did not exist.

In fact, the first official criminal to appear before Justice Jeffcott was James Hoare, who coincidentally also fathered the first European child born in South Australia. He was fined five pounds for stealing a flitch of bacon and Colonel Light, the Surveyor General, who had known him from their long sea journey together to South Australia, paid his fine.

The first purpose-built court house was a timber structure in Whitmore Square. It was very unpopular with judges who complained of the dust on their clothes. This building burnt down within a few years and judicial cases were heard, temporarily, in the pits of the Old Queens Theatre off Currie Street.

The present building was begun in 1847 and finally completed in 1850, making it the oldest standing building on Victoria Square. Built of sandstone with a Doric portico, it was designed by Richard Lambeth and used as the Supreme Court until 1873, the Local and Insolvency courts until 1891 and since then, as the Magistrates Court.

A touch of irony marked the opening of this courthouse. The builder under-quoted and refused to hand over the keys until the extra money was paid. The government refused to pay more than the quoted sum, so the Solicitor-General and his men had to break into the new Courthouse to gain access when it was completed.

Up in recent years, the stone around the footings have had to be replaced due to salt-damp but it has been difficult to match the new footings with the original. Modern extensions have also been added to the rear of the building.

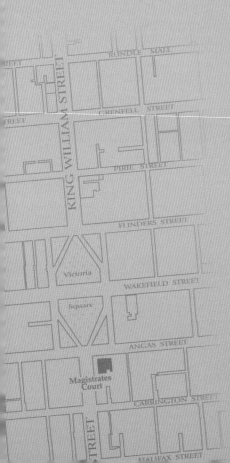

ADELAIDE RAILWAY STATION › North Terrace

WA Webb, Commissioner of Railways from 1922-30, would no doubt turn in his grave if he could see the fortunes being won and lost at roulette wheels and blackjack tables in his railway station. However, few buildings illustrate the precarious fortunes of the transport system more vividly than the Adelaide Railway Station.

The first government-owned steam railway in the British Empire operated here in 1856, between the original Adelaide station on this site and Port Adelaide. A hotel was built opposite the stations at each end of the line; the Terminus, now renamed the Strathmore Hotel, still stands on North Terrace opposite the station. As the population increased and rail services improved, the small single-storied Adelaide station with its arched portico was extended at either end and had a second storey added in the 1870s, to cope with increased traffic.

Railways boomed in the last part of the nineteenth century but the introduction of trams and motor cars took a hefty toll. As part of an attempt to revitalise the rail system, Commissioner Webb commissioned the present Railway Station, with its grand Marble Hall and concourse. Controversy raged about the vast expense versus the much-needed employment the building would provide in the difficult postwar years. The new building was completed in 1926 but the cost of a building of this scale was the final straw for the treasury and South Australia slid into the depression two years ahead, between 1921-23. Ironically, sixty years later the Adelaide Casino opened in the northern end of the building, incorporating the refurbished Marble Hall (popular as a film set—including the ballroom scene in *Gallipoli*—and a party venue) as its entrance and has been providing a very healthy income for the state coffers ever since.

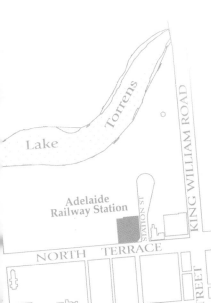

The Adelaide Railway Station is still the city terminus for suburban trains. Constructed of reinforced concrete, it was technically advanced for its time. The design employs classical architectural features, such as egg-and-dart mouldings, impressive Ionic columns and balustrades, which add to the building's sense of history and grandeur.

BOTANIC CHAMBERS ❯ 301–307 North Terrace

Adelaide's magnificent Botanic Gardens occupy the land at the eastern end of North Terrace. Directly opposite the delicately wrought-iron gates which frame the entrance to the gardens is the Botanic Hotel which stands on the corner of North and East Terraces. Adjacent to the hotel are the Botanic Chambers built in the style of traditional Victorian terrace houses.

Businessman Richard Vaughan financed the construction of the Botanic Hotel and Chambers with the profits from the sale of the East End Market in 1875. He built the Botanic Hotel in 1876–67 next to the market site, as a restaurant and family hotel and significantly enlarged it in 1883.

The original architect was Michael McMullen, who also designed the three-storey row of seven terrace houses constructed at the same time along North Terrace and the attached shops and houses along East Terrace.

Traditionally providing accommodation in association with the hotel, each terrace house had twelve rooms including a bathroom and was completely separate from the next, externally demonstrated by the decorative pilasters separating each house. The balconies afforded wonderful views and, no doubt, a bird's-eye view of the Botanic Gardens. The hotel was very similar in style with an additional storey and twenty-five rooms. Originally unadorned, the hotel's tiered balconies were added in 1897, giving it its present appearance. In more recent times the terraces have become doctors' and dentists' rooms, serviced apartments and privately owned townhouses.

Once a bookseller and a grocer, Vaughan also became a property developer, building the Kensington Hotel and Romilly House, on the corner of North Terrace and Hackney Road, hoping to lease it as a school. However his speculative building spree ended when his bank foreclosed in 1879. Richard Vaughan had always been a risk-taker but his luck finally ran out.

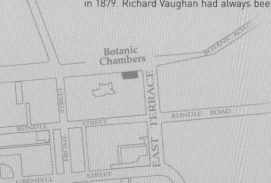

MENZ BISCUIT FACTORY › 82 Wakefield Street

Buildings in the city of Adelaide have a rich diversity of styles and uses, from grand and important government institutions to humble workers' cottages. Often overlooked, however, are the solid industrial structures such as warehouses and factories which, because of the lack of glamour associated with their uses, are often undervalued for their architecture and contributions to the streetscapes.

One such building is the former Menz Biscuit Factory, now converted to offices, in Wakefield Street. John and Magdalena Menz first occupied a shop and a bakery in Wakefield Street in the early 1850s. John died in 1860 and Magdalena went on to run the business until their elder son, William, took over in 1867 and was later joined by his brother August. As the business grew, biscuit production increased, the original grocery trade ceased and new equipment was installed for increased confectionary production.

The buildings also grew and this two-storey bluestone factory, constructed in 1878 in Italianate style, includes decorative cast-iron balconettes. This elaborate detailing reflects obvious confidence in the success of the business at the time. Further sections were added in 1912 and again in 1946.

W Menz and Co. Ltd became a private company in 1935 and eventually a public company in 1951. It was at this time the operations of the biscuit factory moved from the original Wakefield Street premises to the western suburbs in 1953 and the offices were transferred in the 1960s. When W Menz and Co. Ltd became part of Arnott Motteram Menz in 1979 the decision was taken to move the confectionary manufacturing operations (including the enrobing of chocolate biscuits) out to the western suburbs too.

Internal alterations to the factory have been extensive, including restoration after a fire almost gutted the building in the 1980s. Renovations since then have restored the balconettes and the shopfront to the important Divett Place corner and added unusual balconies to the Wakefield Street entrance. The Legal Services Commission now occupies the former Menz Biscuit Factory.

NEWMARKET HOTEL › corner North and West Terraces

The Newmarket Hotel occupies Town Acre No. 1, the first piece of land to be officially surveyed by Colonel William Light, Surveyor General of Adelaide. A cairn on the lawn opposite the hotel marks the site from which the survey of the city began, on 11 January, 1837.

This elegant three-storey hotel was built in 1883 for licensee Francis Badman. It replaced a humble single-storey building known as the Newmarket Inn, established in 1847 and so named because Adelaide's first cattle markets were located across the road, near the River Torrens. The *Register* newspaper of 17 July 1883 stated, 'The old building was a relic of the past primitive days but the new one means luxury and progress'.

Daniel Garlick designed the Newmarket Hotel which is built of square-cut sandstone and is a fine example of a Victorian hotel, with its decorated balconies and faces carved into the keystones in the windows. A feature of the main entrance hall off North Terrace is a free-standing spiral staircase carved from cedar.

The Newmarket is one of three hotels in Adelaide which claim to have invented the 'butcher' glass, for a medium-sized beer. Folklore has it that the butchers who worked at the markets were too thirsty to be satisfied with a small glass, known as a 'pony', but too busy to stay long enough to drink a larger schooner or a pint; hence the medium-size butcher glass (now agreed to be 170 ml), distinctively South Australian.

In the 1920s, one of the hotel's colourful owners was Bert Edwards, widely thought to be the illegitimate son of Charles Cameron Kingston, a former Premier of South Australia. Edwards was a champion of the underdog, a philanthropist and unfortunately a pederast who began his commercial life selling ice-creams in the market and went on to become a city councillor and state politician. When Labour won government in 1921, he had the task of formulating South Australia's first probation system but in 1930 he was jailed himself for two-and-a-half years for sodomy. During this time, the Newmarket Hotel was issued with a foreclosure order, enabling a new owner to purchase the hotel. When Edwards won back his City Council seat in 1948, the Lord Mayor, John McLeay, proclaimed, 'He has been elected and we must accept him with our backs to the wall'.

The Newmarket Hotel is still a prominent landmark in the city of Adelaide, occupying an important corner on the approach into the city from Port Adelaide and the north-western suburbs.

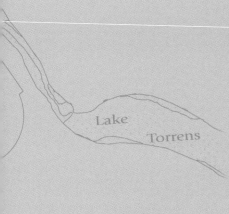

WEST'S COFFEE PALACE › 104–120 Hindley Street

The dramatic upstairs facade of West's Coffee Palace is often unnoticed by passers-by in Hindley Street; the modernised shopfronts at street level bear no hint of the eclectic architecture and its intricate adornments above.

West's Coffee Palace was built in 1903 as the Austral Stores for prominent businessman Leopold Conrad on the site of earlier shops he owned; the architect was Albert Conrad, his elder son. The red brick facade with cream rendered dressings and embellishments is similar to the Adelaide Fruit and Produce Exchange, built the following year. Hindley Street in those days was an important commercial and residential street characterized by increasingly substantial buildings, many with wide balconies.

Austral Stores comprised twelve shops, with the yards at the rear used for Mr Conrad's butchering business. Five years later, Grant's Coffee Palace which had been across the road, moved into the Austral Stores, thus beginning a tradition of Coffee Palace occupancy.

Coffee Palaces were temperance hotels, the forerunners of unlicensed restaurants. They were very popular in South Australia in the late nineteenth and early twentieth centuries; a strong temperance movement resulted in the introduction of six o'clock closing at all hotels during the First World War, a law that remained until the 1960s. John West was proprietor of the Federal Coffee Palace in North Terrace, which was demolished to make way for the Grosvenor Hotel. So in 1919, West took over the management of this Coffee Palace in Hindley Street, changed its name to West's and it operated until 1979. It did have a wine licence and restaurant during the 1930s. The ornate shopfronts and verandahs were replaced in the 1960s.

With valuable restoration work now completed on the upper storey with its twin three-storey towers and extravagant embellishments, West's Coffee Palace remains a significant feature of the Hindley Street skyline.

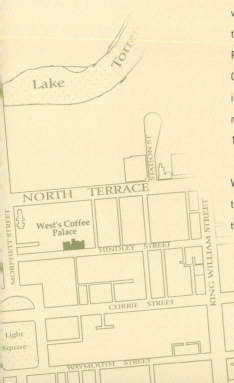

COLONIAL STORE › off North Terrace
Behind Art Gallery of South Australia

This small but beautifully proportioned building was quite prominently placed when it was built in 1867 next to the Barracks and Armoury facing onto North Terrace. It is now located immediately behind the Art Gallery of South Australia and used as part of the Gallery.

Built as the New Colonial Store, it became home to the State Archives in 1919 and major renovations at this time saw the pitched roof of the porch removed to make way for a triple window. Dormer windows in the roof were removed and the building took on something of a doll's house appearance, with its scalloped fascia boards following the pitch of the roof.

In the early 1980s, the building was completely restored; the pitched roof on the porch once again replaced the upper windows and the salt-damp, which afflicts most city buildings, was leeched from the bluestone. The old Adelaide brick quoins near ground level were completely replaced. The building's uses have changed considerably over the years. In 1969, it became the South Australian Historical Museum, then later the Gallery of South Australian Art and since the extensions to the Art Gallery in 1996, the Radford Auditorium. The building is now named after long-time Gallery Director Ron Radford and is used extensively for talks and lectures.

ROMAN CATHOLIC CHAPEL › West Terrace Cemetery, West Terrace

The land for a cemetery in the parklands adjacent to West Terrace was designated in Colonel Light's original plan and the earliest burials took place there in 1837. The remains of many famous pioneers are to be found in West Terrace Cemetery. Among them are world-renowned musician and composer Percy Grainger; George Strickland Kingston, the first Colonial Architect; his son, Charles Cameron Kingston, Premier of South Australia and known as the father of Federation and Carl Linger, who composed the music for the *Song of Australia*, our first official national anthem. Coincidentally, Caroline Carleton who composed the lyrics for the *Song of Australia* lived for a time in the caretaker's house at the main gates of the West Terrace Cemetery.

The octagonal Roman Catholic Chapel was built in 1870 to the design of Edward John Woods and has the distinction of being the only Gothic revival building in Adelaide with gargoyles. Built of bluestone with freestone dressings, each of the buttresses is surmounted by a carved gargoyle, taking the form of medieval grotesques with bat-like wings forming spouts for the flow of water from the gutters. Sadly, most of them have been severely defaced by vandals, as have many of the headstones in the cemetery. The timber and iron spire creates a particularly decorative silhouette on the cemetery landscape.

The chapel was built as a memorial to the Very Reverend John Smyth, the Catholic Vicar-General of South Australia, who died in 1870; his remains lie beneath the chapel foundations. It also contains other remains including those of Bishop Sheil, who opened the chapel in October 1871 but who unfortunately died within six months of this event.

The Roman Catholic Chapel was included by the Australian Heritage Commission on the Register of the National Estate in 1978.

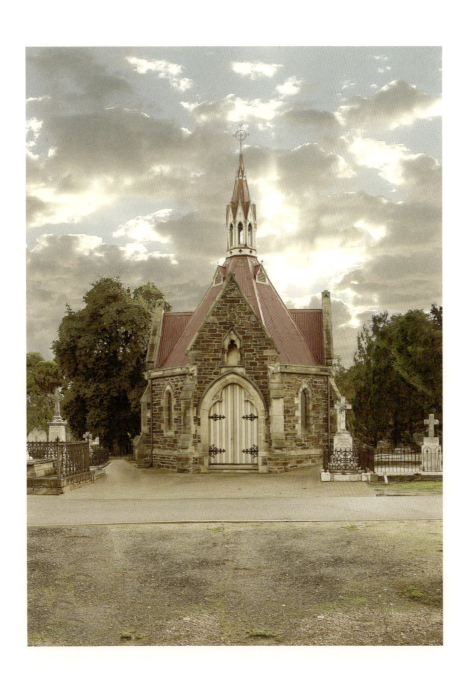

AYERS HOUSE › 288 North Terrace

Ayers House, designed by George Strickland Kingston, grew from a humble cottage into one of Adelaide's most elegant Regency houses. The original cottage was built in 1845 for Robert Thornber, who sold the property a year later to Hindley Street chemist William Paxton and one of the founders of the South Australian Mining Company. Paxton extended the land and added stables, a coach-house and courtyard before returning to England in 1855.

The house was leased to Henry Ayers, then Managing Director of the South Australian Mining Company, who made a fortune from copper mining at Burra Burra in the state's north; in 1845 he had bought some of the original five pound shares which were worth £225 by 1851. He enlarged the house to include a library, upstairs bedrooms, a ballroom and a formal dining room. The matching bow windows with curved glass and louvered shutters were characteristic of Kingston's designs and Ayers House is one of the few remaining examples in Adelaide.

Henry Ayers was elected Premier of South Australia five times and knighted in 1872. Ayers Rock (now renamed Uluru) was named after him by his friend, explorer William Gosse. The house was the scene of lavish social activity and grand state occasions until Sir Henry's death in 1897.

From 1914, Ayers House became an entertainment centre known as Austral Gardens, with an open-air theatre and dance hall, the Palais Royal. During the depression years of the 1920s, the government purchased the building for a nurses' home for the Royal Adelaide Hospital across the road, using the dining room as a dormitory. The nurses claimed the house was haunted. After major renovations in 1972, Ayers House was opened to the public. The central section became a National Trust museum, the eastern end a formal restaurant named Henry Ayers and the old coach-house become a less formal eatery.

The grounds, library, elegant dining room and ballroom, restored to their former glory, are popular for weddings and private functions, just as they were a century ago.

DIMORA > 120 East Terrace

While the minor streets of South Adelaide were lined with single and double-fronted workers' cottages and the major streets with more substantial cottages and villas owned by business and professional people, the terraces facing the parklands were dotted with the mansions of the wealthy.

Dimora, meaning 'abode' or 'house' in Italian, is an exceptionally fine example of an Adelaide bluestone mansion, built in 1882 for Harry Ayers, son of Sir Henry and Lady Ayers who lived at Ayers House on North Terrace. Harry Ayers died in 1905 but his family continued to live in Dimora until 1940.

Dimora was designed by architect William McMinn and its features, typical of the period, include wide bay windows, exquisitely fine cast-iron lace and double verandah posts. McMinn, with his characteristic eye for detail, designed the bluestone front fence and iron-lace entrance gates to complement the house.

Described in a real estate advertisement a hundred years later as 'unquestionably the finest residence of its type in Adelaide...ideally suited as a grand private house, consulate or similar', it then boasted nine main rooms including a sitting room, morning room, dining room, study-library, day room, master suite with dressing room and private bathroom, two other bedrooms, cellar room, kitchen, pantry-utility room, main bathroom and cloakroom.

Dimora has since been converted into apartments and its grounds subdivided for townhouse development. Sadly, a hundred-year-old wisteria arbor was destroyed during the building work and has been replaced by a gazebo in the side garden.

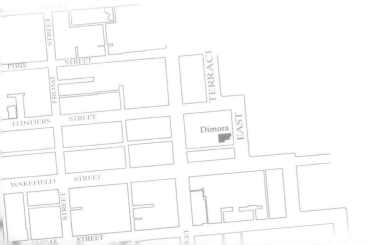

MOUNTED POLICE BARRACKS › North Terrace
Behind South Australian Museum

Tucked away behind the South Australian Museum on North Terrace, this remarkable colonial building was, for much of this century, familiar only to museum staff and students of nearby Adelaide University.

However its complete restoration in 1986, as part of the State's 150th birthday celebrations, brought the Mounted Police Barracks out of hiding with its proud facelift and caused many local residents to marvel at this hidden treasure.

Following the casual sighting of a Russian warship in the Gulf of St Vincent in the early 1850s, the colonists went into panic. Volunteers were hastily enrolled and a military establishment, designed around a quadrangle, was built in 1855 on North Terrace, to house the troops. The quadrangle was entered through two imposing stone arches with iron gates, one of which still stands today.

This western wing of limestone began as a single-storey building with a slate roof, built as police barracks, horse stables and gaol cells. A second floor was added in 1882, with external wooden stairs and balcony. After the mounted police vacated these premises in 1921, this building was used as a teachers' training college before being converted to the Children's Library, the first in Australia, in 1927. It has more recently housed a museum of South Australian police history and memorabilia and is now part of the History Trust and the Migration Museum.

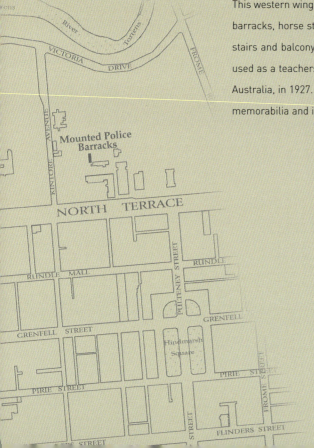

ADELAIDE TOWN HALL > King William Street

At the time of its completion in 1866, the Adelaide Town Hall was described as the largest municipal building south of the equator. The foundation stone for the first (central) section was laid by the Governor, Sir Dominic Daly, in 1863. Designed by two of Adelaide's most respected architects, Edmund Wright and Edward Woods, the building was officially opened three years later.

Edmund Wright, himself Mayor of Adelaide in 1859, had travelled in Europe and was obviously impressed with classical Italian architecture and incorporated this into the design of Adelaide's Town Hall.

The tower was named after Prince Albert, consort of Queen Victoria; their faces adorn the arches leading to the main entrance. The balcony and tower provide an arched entranceway which extends over the footpath, a feature that is unique in Adelaide. The faces in the other arches are thought to be those of fifteenth century artists and designers admired by the architects. Across King William Street, the tower on the General Post Office is named after Queen Victoria; although they do not match, they are in some respects, twin towers, providing a commanding entrance to Victoria Square from the north. The City of Adelaide's coat of arms on the Albert tower has a lion representing England and a kangaroo representing Australia, above a Latin inscription translating as 'United for the Common Good'.

The central section of the Town Hall and the tower are built of freestone. The sections added later on either side, although built of different materials and designed by other architects, are complementary. The section to the right, nearer Victoria Square, was the Prince Alfred Hotel until the 1950s, when it was incorporated into the Town Hall as Prince Alfred Chambers. The addition to the left was built in 1874 and known as Eagle Chambers. The Town Hall clock was donated by Sir Lavington Bonython (a member of the City Council for forty-three years including two terms as Mayor and three terms as Lord Mayor) and put in motion by him at three o'clock on 20 February 1935.

Queen Adelaide is well represented in the Town Hall with a room on the ground floor bearing her name since Queen Elizabeth II presented a portrait of Queen Adelaide in 1953. In 1980 a bronze statue by New Zealand born sculptor Lindsay Daen was added in the entrance hall.

Many Adelaide residents recall standing in King William Street below the balconies of the Adelaide Town Hall to celebrate New Year's Eve, homecomings of sporting heroes and visiting celebrities honoured with civic receptions. No-one old enough to be there in the 1963 could forget the day The Beatles came to town and Adelaide played host to 300 000 screaming fans, the largest number to gather for a Beatles welcome anywhere in the world.

QUEEN'S CHAMBERS > Pirie Street

Queen's Chambers, now part of the Adelaide Town Hall complex, was built in 1869 as a suite of offices in quite a different style from its neighbours, Gladstone Chambers and the early Pirie Street Wesleyan church. Edmund Wright, the Town Hall architect, had stipulated the kinds of designs and building materials to be used in all buildings on the Town Hall Acre. This section of the land was leased to GW Cotton, who built the beautifully proportioned Queen's Chambers and used part of it for his land-broking office. Architects were, once again, William McMinn and Daniel Garlick.

Queen's Chambers' cantilevered balcony displays one of the earliest examples of cast-iron lacework in Adelaide. Many of Adelaide's later, more substantial buildings, from hotels to private homes, have since become renowned for their decorative iron lace but it did not become popular until the late 1870s and well into the 1880s.

Queen's Chambers' facade has been largely unchanged since it was built, although at one stage a barber's shop occupied half the street-level frontage. Fortunately, these alterations were easily removed and it remains, externally, one of the city's most elegant commercial buildings. The interior has changed dramatically, since the building was incorporated into the offices of the Corporation of the City of Adelaide in the 1970s.

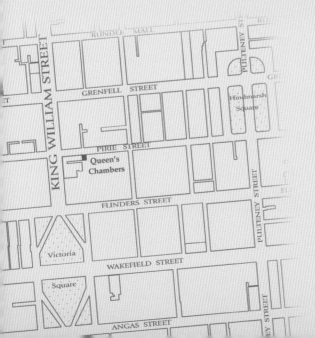

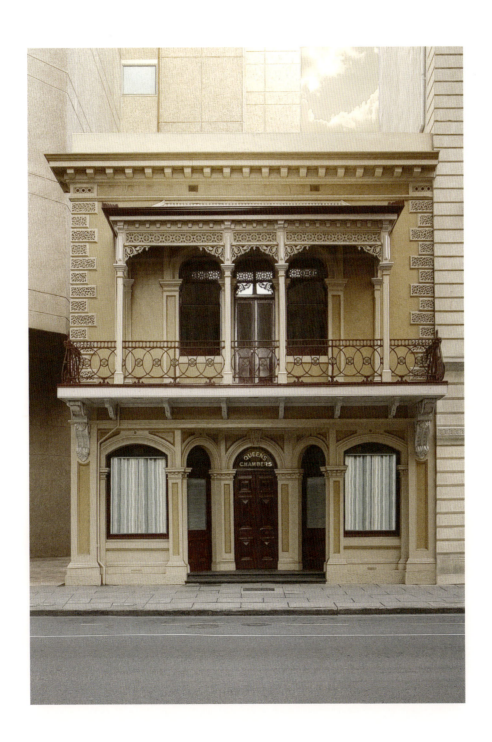

HINDLEY STREET OFFICES > 224 Hindley Street

This Hindley Street office complex, now owned by the Australian Institute of Management, has a simple elegance. The interior is equally well-designed with wood panelling and decorative wrought iron. It was built during the war years and completed in 1941 as the administrative headquarters for the South Australian Brewing Company. Extensions were added in 1956.

The South Australian Brewing Company was formed in 1888, an amalgamation of various breweries, including the West End and Kent Town and originally named the South Australian Brewing, Malting and Wine and Spirit Company Ltd. The name was shortened in 1893.

Much of the company's success was attributed to the great brewing skills of Thomas Nation, the chief brewer for the first half of this century. The South Australian Brewing Company moved its offices to Thebarton in 1984 and sold this building to the Australian Institute of Management – South Australia.

The work of prominent architect Kenneth Milne, the offices are built in the Georgian style, although with an Italianate flavour; the brickwork is highlighted by finely detailed artificial stone dressings. This building is of particular interest as it reflects a time when architects began to interpret rather than copy particular styles. It is unusual in Adelaide for a building of this type and scale to be constructed almost entirely of brick with such restrained adornments.

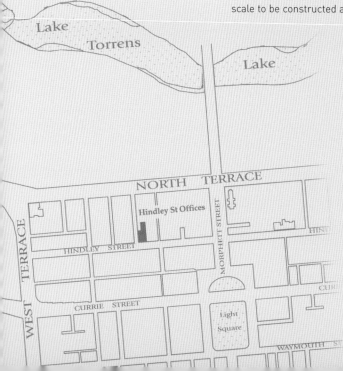

BONYTHON HALL › University of Adelaide, North Terrace

Bonython Hall could easily be mistaken for an English university hall. Visible the whole length of Pulteney Street from as far back as the south parklands, it is a glorious gift of one of Adelaide's most generous benefactors.

During the early years of the depression, Sir Langdon Bonython, then owner of *The Advertiser* newspaper and a great champion of education, offered to fill the breach by paying the salaries of South Australia's teachers when the treasury was unable to do so. In 1930, the government was able to repay the loan. Sir Langdon had announced some years earlier that he would give money to the University of Adelaide to build a great hall but at the time the university did not own all the land he had chosen for the site. He wanted the university to have the type of hall to be found in Oxford or Cambridge universities.

His donation of £40 000 enabled the Great Hall to go ahead and the University made up the total cost. But Sir Langdon put two stipulations on his bequest. The first was that the building must be placed plumb at the end of Pulteney Street to prevent any further talk of extending Pulteney Street through the grounds of the University to the Zoo. The second was that the hall must have a sloping floor. Sir Langdon was a strict Methodist who disapproved of dancing and he insisted that no dancing should occur in his hall.

The medieval-Gothic style of Bonython Hall belies its youth. Completed in 1936 to coincide with South Australia's 150th birthday celebrations, it is built of Murray Bridge limestone, with a Willunga slate roof, jarrah and pine floors and an elaborately decorated ceiling. The supervising architect was Walter Bagot who was meticulous about detail and craftsmanship. Its interior walls, panelled in Australian oak, are lined with portraits of Chancellors and Vice- Chancellors of the University. The hall is used for graduations and other ceremonial occasions.

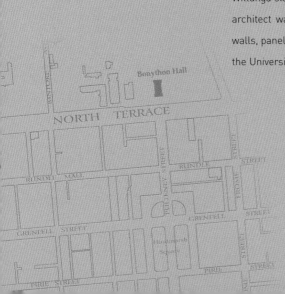

ST FRANCIS XAVIER CATHEDRAL > Wakefield Street

Like the great cathedrals of Europe, St Francis Xavier Cathedral was built in many different stages, according to the fortunes of the colony. Work began on the foundations in 1851 yet its spire on the north-western corner was only completed 140 years later in the 1990s by the grace of a generous private donation.

The first section, the small 'parish church' at the southern end, was completed in 1858 to the design of an English architect, Charles Hansom. A competition for the best design had been announced a few years earlier but the winning architect, Richard Lambeth, downed tools and joined the rush to the Victorian goldfields and it seems he never returned.

Some of the finest English architects of the time, Pugin & Pugin, were involved in the design of the central section, which was built in the 1880s under the supervision of Adelaide architect Edward Woods, with Gothic arches and buttresses facing Victoria Square. A small front porch was added as the entrance from Wakefield Street.

The northern section of the nave and the tower was completed between 1922 and 1926, giving the cathedral a much grander facade and entrance, with a temporary little cap where the spire would later complete the tower. Walter Bagot was the architect. The building is of bluestone with rendered dressings.

There is some irony attached to the siting of the Catholic Cathedral in Victoria Square. Colonel Light, Adelaide's first Surveyor General, had marked with an X the spot on his map where he intended the Anglican Cathedral to be built; in true English town-planning tradition, it was to be in the centre of Victoria Square, that is, in the centre of the city.

When the first Anglican Bishop arrived in 1847 and attempted to claim this site for his cathedral, Adelaide's large non-conformist population banded together and flatly refused. After a prolonged battle which ended up in the Supreme Court, St Peter's Anglican Cathedral was finally built across the river in North Adelaide. With a stretch of lawn occupying the land to its west, St Francis Xavier Catholic Cathedral is now a prominent feature of Victoria Square.

MITCHELL BUILDING › University of Adelaide, North Terrace

This fine example of modern Gothic architecture was the first structure built for the University of Adelaide on its own grounds. The university was inaugurated at a meeting in 1876 and women made up thirty-three of the first sixty students.

Sir Walter Watson Hughes, whose imposing statue sits in front of the Mitchell Building, provided the first major donation to the University in 1872. He had made his fortune when copper was discovered on his sheep station at Walla Waroo, later named Wallaroo, on York Peninsula. The substantial donations of Sir Walter and Sir Thomas Elder also enabled the University to attract top academics from overseas, among them philosopher William Mitchell, after whom this building is named, who served on the University Council for fifty-two years.

The Mitchell Building is probably the finest example of modern Gothic architecture still standing in Adelaide. On close inspection, the detailing is extraordinary: two different shades of slate in alternating rows adorn the roof beneath an ornamental iron casting and 35 foot (10.6 metres) turret designed for ventilation, as well as aesthetics. Columns of red Scottish stone embellish the upper-storey windows and form pillars at the entrances of the open stone-porch. Exquisite carvings garnish the cornices and bands of darker tinted stone are added to accentuate the arches of the windows.

Today the Mitchell Building houses, among other things, the Museum of Classical Archaeology, a collection of almost 800 artefacts including Egyptian and Mesopotamian pottery and over 1100 coins.

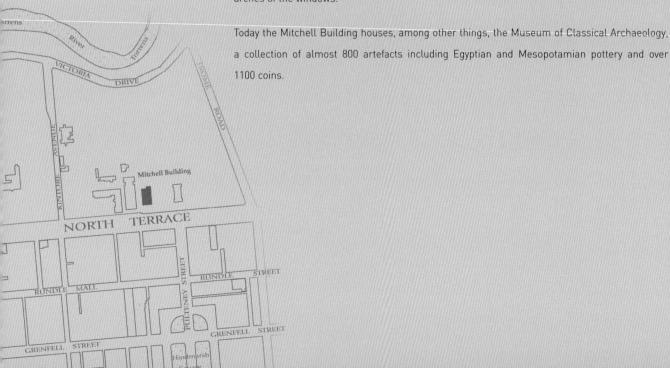

NORTH LODGE ❯ Botanic Gardens, North Terrace

After several failed attempts, Adelaide's Botanic Gardens were established on North Terrace in 1855, on forty acres of land previously used for grazing police horses. The first Director, George Francis, was appointed that same year and the gardens were officially opened to the public in August 1857. The layout was strongly influenced by Kew Gardens in England and has not been substantially altered, although considerably more land has since been added.

In addition to the botanic collections, the gardens were originally also home to a variety of caged birds and animals, numbering well over 500 before they were transferred to the zoo when it opened in 1883.

The North Lodge was built in 1867 as the head gardener's cottage. An attractive asymmetrical building, its style is that of a typical gatehouse found on an English country estate. While some of its features such as the chimneys, fascia boards and the narrow bay window in the gable-wall are Gothic-inspired, it is a colonial design later emulated in the Adelaide bluestone villa. It would typically have had two bedrooms, a living room and a kitchen with an outside water closet in the backyard, possibly a shed and a covered verandah.

The North Lodge is located near the rear gate of the Botanic Gardens, off Botanic Park, and now houses a souvenir shop.

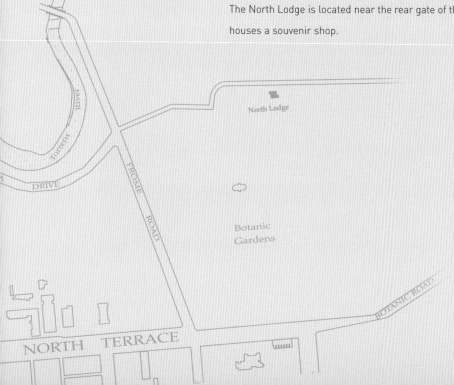

ADELAIDE GAOL › 18 Gaol Road, off Port Road

Within a year of settlement, it was apparent that there was some urgency to build a secure place to hold prisoners in the colony; the temporary tents and wooden structure known as the Stone Jug preceding this building were filthy and escape was easy. However South Australia's second governor, Governor Gawler, sent the colony bankrupt by ordering the building of this unnecessarily large and costly gaol—it cost £32 000—and a grand residence for himself, within three years of European settlement.

Based on an English design, the Adelaide Gaol is the only radially designed gaol still remaining in Australia today. It was designed by George Strickland Kingston, Colonial Architect, with guard towers, hanging tower and substantial surrounding walls in 'Norman Gothic' style and opened in 1841. A two-storey classical Victorian administrative building forms the entrance to the gaol but the cell blocks with their romantic towers and heavy stone castellations are the most formidable and impressive parts of the building. The government actually drew the line at all the embellishments planned for the gaol and one of the towers is still without its castellations. The bricks on the parapets around the top of the tower walls are free-standing without mortar. The parapets would have literally fallen like a ton of bricks on anyone attempting escape.

In December, 1854, over two thousand people gathered at the Adelaide Gaol to watch a public hanging. Parents lifted their children up to give them a better view and it turned into such a gala occasion that the public was banned from future hangings. Over the course of its life, the Adelaide Gaol housed more than three hundred thousand inmates, including the luckless Elizabeth Woolcott who achieved the dubious honour of being the first woman to be hanged in the Adelaide Gaol for the murder of her husband. Squizzy Taylor, a Melbourne gangster killed in a shoot out in 1927 and the subject of a 1984 film of the same name, was also believed to have languished for a time in the Adelaide Gaol.

The gaol was decommissioned in 1988; it now houses a visitor centre and museum and is one of the most unusual venues in South Australia for cocktail parties, murder dinners, theme parties and banquets. The Adelaide Gaol Preservation Society exists to ensure that this significant heritage site remains an accessible aspect of Adelaide's early history.

ALBERT BRIDGE › Frome Road

The Aboriginal name for the river that flowed through the centre of Adelaide was *Karrawirraparri*, meaning 'red gum forest river'. With European settlement it was renamed after Robert Torrens, a member of the British Parliament at the time of settlement and the Chairman of the South Australian Colonisation Commission. His son Robert, one of the founders of South Australia and for a time Premier is best remembered for steering the Torrens Land Title through Parliament.

Early attempts to build bridges across the River Torrens failed miserably; most were washed away when the river flooded in bad weather, leaving the citizens stranded. All the present bridges in the city have replaced at least one or, in some cases, several flimsier versions.

The Albert Bridge, on Frome Road near the Adelaide Zoo, is the oldest surviving bridge spanning the Torrens. An earlier structure, known as the Old Frome Bridge, was washed away in the late 1840s, causing the citizens to cross at the city bridge for thirty years. The new bridge, opened in 1879, was designed by John Grainger, father of composer Percy Grainger. *The Advertiser* of 8th May 1879 quoted the Mayor, Mr William Buik as saying the bridge was named after "the illustrious husband of our beloved Queen". Although Prince Albert had died 18 years earlier, Queen Victoria mourned him for the remainder of her life.

Constructed on cylindrical cast-iron piers filled with concrete, three parallel scalloped-girders hold the roadway, originally made of compacted metal on buckle plates but replaced in 1956 with a concrete slab and bitumen. The decorative cast-iron handrails and lamp standards, ordered from England, are typical of the period and add a decided elegance to this otherwise very practical and enduring piece of engineering.

The best way to appreciate the bridge's riveted undercarriage is via a cruise or a paddleboat under the bridge. Although the river no longer flows, it is always a busy place for rowers, paddle-boaters, walkers, cyclists and families of ducks.

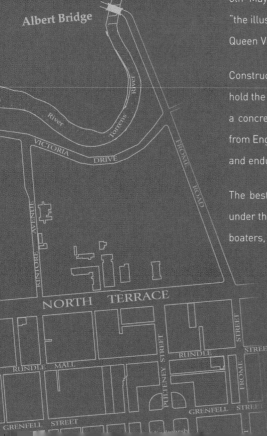

GLOSSARY ›

Balconette: miniature balcony

Besser block: concrete masonry unit, a substitute for stone or brick

Buttress: a structure of wood, stone or brick built against a wall to support it

Cantilever: bracket projecting horizontally from a wall to support a balcony, cornice or similar structure

Cararra marble: fine stone mined from Cararra in Tuscany, Italy which has supplied marble since Roman times, including the stone used in Michelangelo's famous statue of the Pieta and David

Castellations: indented parapets or battlements, originating on city walls or medieval castles, where portions of the parapet have been cut out at intervals to allow the shooting of arrows or other missiles

Chancel: the eastern part of a church, separated from the other parts by a screen or railing

Cupola: a dome-shaped ornamental structure located on top of a larger roof or dome. The word comes from the Italian, meaning a 'small tub'. Cupola can refer to the entire main roof of a tower or spire or a smaller structure which sits on top of the main roof

Dormer windows: projecting vertical windows in the sloping roof of a building

Dressings: ornamental decorations or finishes on a wall

Dry Creek stone: stone from a quarry at Dry Creek on the northern outskirts of Adelaide

Egg-and-dart moulding: decorative pattern moulded in rounded half-egg shapes interspersed with downward pointed arrow or dart shapes; often used on internal or external plaster cornices and wooden picture frames

Footings: a projecting course or courses at the foundation of a wall

Freestone: fine-grained sandstone or limestone, easily cut or sawn

Gargoyle: a grotesque spout, representing an animal or human figure, projecting from the gutter of a building to carry the rainwater clear of the walls

Ionic columns: Ionic is one of the three orders of Grecian architecture (Doric, Ionic, Corinthian) originating in Ionia, the south-west coastland of Asia Minor in 6th century BC and characterized by a pair of spiral curves on the capital (the ornamental crown of the column)

Mansard roof: named after the French architect Francois Mansard (1598 -1666) this term refers to a form of curb-roof, in which each face of the roof has two slopes, the lower one steeper than the other

Pilasters: shallow ornamental square or rectangular columns erected against a wall

Quoins: masonry cornerstones forming the external angle on a wall or building

Reinforced concrete: concrete with metal bars, gratings or wire embedded in it for added strength

Rococo: lavish decoration often with shell or scroll-work, florid and ornate

String-courses: a distinctive moulding or course running horizontally across the face of a building or around it

Transept: the cross-wise section of a cruciform church (shaped like a cross) and the two arms either side of the nave or body of the church

Vestry: a room or part of a church in which the vestments are kept and the clergy or choir robe for a service

Window mullions: frames which divide adjacent panes of glass. In the past, mullions were necessary because it was not possible to produce sufficiently large panes. Today, they are mainly used for decorative purposes

NOTES > ARCHITECTS

Walter Hervey Bagot

Walter Bagot is one of the first architects to be born and trained in the colony (although he did complete his training overseas) who had also worked with the masters of nineteenth century colonial architecture. He was the grandson of both Captain Charles Bagot who made a fortune discovering copper at Kapunda and of Sir Henry Ayers. Bagot was articled to Edward Woods and later joined him in partnership, creating the firm Woods Bagot. With a scholarly interest in art and architecture, he was noted for his attention to architectural history and detail. He designed a 60 metre spire for St Francis Xavier Cathedral in the early 1920s but due to the onset of the depression, it was to be seventy years before the spire appeared. He also designed Elder House in Currie Street; Bonython Hall, the Barr Smith Library and the gates of the Mitchell Building at the University of Adelaide and the exquisite Cunningham Memorial Chapel at the Convent of Mercy in Angas Street. Bagot lived in the elegant townhouse at 261 North Terrace (see page 12) from 1906-1926 and during this time, co-initiated the state's first School of Architecture with friend and later partner, Louis Laybourne-Smith.

William Bennett Hays

Hays was appointed Surveyor of Main Roads and Clerk of Works and Architecture within twelve months of arriving in South Australia in 1849. The following year he became Colonial Architect and Supervisor of Works during which time he became interested in iron jetties. He oversaw construction of the railway line between Adelaide and Port Adelaide in 1853. The following year he was censured for 'lack of intelligence and zeal' and took a year's leave, ordering materials for construction of the Glenelg jetty while away in London. In 1856 he was dismissed as Colonial Architect for accepting a gift from the contractor of the Port Willunga jetty. Old Parliament House on North Terrace is his only surviving building.

Henry James Cowell

Born at Clarendon, South Australia in 1855, he began his career as a builder with firms such as Brown & Thompson, while studying architectural drawing at the Adelaide School of Design. In 1875 he established his building and timber business in Norwood but after eleven years he retired from the firm and bought a fruit garden at Lockleys. Two years later he began practising as an architect, designing beautiful homes in Victoria Avenue, Unley Park, large city warehouses and several institute buildings. He is best remembered for having designed and supervised the building of the Adelaide Fruit and Produce Exchange building at the corner of East Terrace and Grenfell Street.

James Cumming

James Cumming arrived from Glasgow in 1846 with his father and brother and founded a thriving architectural practice. His designs included Draper Memorial Church (later renamed the Apostolic Church) in Gilbert Street for the Wesleyan Methodists, Bethlehem Lutheran Church in Flinders Street and the Adelaide and Gay's Arcades in Rundle Street. Employing Welsh architect Edward Davies, Cumming's firm won a number of important design competitions including Padthaway in the south-east of South Australia, the National Mutual Life Building in Victoria Square and the Julia Farr Centre (formerly known as the Home for Incurables).

Michael Egan

Melbourne architect, Michael Egan won the design competition for the Torrens Building (government offices) in Victoria Square. His design was constructed under the auspices of the Architect in Chief Edward Woods. He was also awarded second prize in a competition for the Mitchell Building at the University of Adelaide but the final role of architect was given to William McMinn who, much to Egan's chagrin, employed many of Egan's designs and ideas.

Daniel Garlick

Born in Gloucester, Garlick came to the new colony in 1837 with his father Moses who set up a building and timber business in North Adelaide with his three sons. In 1850 the family moved north to farm and grow grapes but Daniel had other ideas. Although he had no formal training, he established himself as an architect at Gawler where he constructed some eighty churches and banks in Gawler and nearby townships. In the 1860s he moved to Adelaide and established a practice in Grenfell Street. Later, his son Arthur joined the firm and D Garlick & Son went on to employ the young Kapunda-born architect Herbert Jackman, eventually becoming Garlick, Jackman and Garlick. Daniel Garlick was a city councillor, a founding member of the South Australian Institute of Architects and is best remembered for buildings such as Prince Alfred College in Kent Town, St Barnabas College and the Prince Alfred Hotel, now part of the Adelaide Town Hall.

Edward Angus Hamilton

Arriving in the colony in 1845 with his wife and children, Hamilton entered government service as a draftsman. He was promoted in 1856 to Colonial Architect after William Bennett Hay's dismissal. He resigned to establish a private practice in 1860. With his brother George, he designed the copper smelters at the Copper Triangle of Wallaroo—Moonta—Kadina on Yorke Peninsula. He designed the Treasury Building as new government offices in Victoria Square (currently Medina apartments), the Institute Building on the corner of Kintore Avenue and North Terrace, the central section of Government House, the Port Adelaide Court House, Customs House and Police Station, St Peter's College Chapel and The Adelaide Club.

Charles Hansom

The Roman Catholic son of a Yorkshire joiner, Charles Hansom was an English architect specialising in church architecture with his brother Joseph (who invented the Hansom cab as a sideline). Their work included Plymouth Cathedral and the Jesuit Church in Manchester. Charles Hansom prepared working drawings for St Francis Xavier Cathedral in Adelaide at the request of Adelaide's Bishop Murphy during his visit to London in 1846. Bishop Murphy brought home Hansom's plans and a model for the cathedral but four years later announced a local competition for the design. After Richard Lambeth's design won, Bishop Murphy had the temerity to request revised plans from Hansom which, amazingly, he received.

George Strickland Kingston

Born in County Cork, architect George 'Paddy' Kingston arrived in 1836 as Deputy Surveyor General to Colonel William Light. Soon recognised as ignorant of surveying (our earliest architects were often engineers and surveyors as well) and unpopular for his arrogance and ungentlemanly behaviour, he was sent back to England only a year later, in 1837. The following year he returned and in 1839 was appointed Civil Engineer and Inspector of Public Works, a position that was abruptly terminated in 1840. Kingston then established himself as a private architect and attracted a number of important commissions, including the East Wing of Government House, the Adelaide Gaol and a number of substantial private homes, including a section of Bray House at 60 Hutt Street. Some of Kingston's domestic architecture with his trademark arched entry porches still stand in Adelaide and around the state as a monument to his skilled adaptation of classic traditions to a new colonial style.

Richard Lambeth

Arriving in 1846 from Tasmania, Lambeth took various government roles as Clerk of Works in between advertising his services as civil engineer and architect. His first major commission was the design of the new courthouse in Victoria Square, now the front section of the Magistrates Court. He collaborated with William Weir on a design for the Legislative Council Building (now Old Parliament House) but lost to William Bennett Hays. Lambeth and Weir also submitted separate designs in the competition for St Francis Xavier Cathedral, along with the cream of architects in Adelaide at the time and Lambeth won. He began work on the foundations but in November of 1851, work came to an abrupt halt when Lambeth (and many of the other men in the colony) downed tools to rush to the Victorian goldfields. Lambeth never returned.

George Gavin Lawson

George Gavin Lawson, a rugged Scot, arrived in South Australia in 1921 aged thirty-nine. He had served five-year articles in Edinburgh before emigrating to South Africa where he worked for seven years. In 1911, with David Parr, he unsuccessfully submitted a plan for the competition to design the new Australian capital city, later Canberra, which was advertised internationally. The following year he moved to Queensland. After serving and being wounded in the First World War, he moved to South Australia where his first major project for the Architect in Chief's department was the Dental Hospital on Frome Road in 1922. He later designed the Bice Building for the Royal Adelaide Hospital and in 1924 the Teachers' Training College (Hartley Building) on Kintore Avenue. He also designed the Burnside Town Hall, the Light Horse Memorial at the corner of East and North Terraces and went on to found the well-known firm of Cheeseman, Doley, Neighbour & Raffen. This firm changed its name many times before being listed as a public company in 1961.

William McMinn

Born in County Down, Ireland and brought to South Australia in 1850 by his parents, McMinn became one of the earliest architects of note to be trained in South Australia. He was articled to architect James MacGeorge before joining the service of the Architect in Chief. In 1864, he abandoned architecture to join the first expedition to explore the northern territory as a surveyor, later winning the role of Government Inspector of the Darwin end of the Overland Telegraph which was being built at the time. He returned to Adelaide around 1870, briefly joining the firms of Daniel Garlick and later Edward Woods. McMinn accomplished a lasting legacy in his short life, contributing to the design of the General Post Office, the Supreme Court Building, the Mitchell Building of the University of Adelaide, the Children's Hospital, the Crown and Scepter Hotel, the Austral Hotel and the grand mansions 'Dimora' on East Terrace and 'Mt Brecken' at Victor Harbor.

Michael McMullen

McMullen was an Irish architect and builder who arrived in 1850 and is associated with the design and building of a number of shops and Roman Catholic buildings in Adelaide. He built the second stage of St Francis Xavier Cathedral in Victoria Square, St Lawrence's Church and Priory in North Adelaide to the design of Wright, Woods and Hamilton and he modified the Catholic Bishop's residence on West Terrace. He also built the new East Wing of the Adelaide hospital and he both designed and built the Botanic Hotel and Chambers in North Terrace.

Kenneth Milne

Grandson of well-known Adelaide architect James McGeorge, Milne was born and articled in South Australia. As a child he showed an early aptitude and interest in architecture when he constantly drew houses. He worked in Sydney for three years and returned, brimming with new ideas, to open an office in Adelaide in 1909. However his contemporaries resented his wider experience and work was slow to come in. The Hampshire Hotel in Franklin Street was his first major commission, followed by the famous scoreboard at the Adelaide Oval, familiar to cricket lovers throughout the world. He also designed, in association with New York architect Thomas Lamb, the Metro Theatre in Hindley Street, which opened in 1939 with Jeanette McDonald and Nelson Eddy in *Sweethearts*. After a visit to Britain, he became proficient in the Georgian style and designed the Georgian office building at 230 Pirie Street, the offices for the South Australian Brewing Company in Hindley Street and his own home, 'Sunnyside' in North Adelaide. Milne has been described as one of the finest domestic architects South Australia has ever known.

Pugin & Pugin

August Welby Pugin was the London-born son of a French architect with a practice in Bedford Square. A convert to Roman Catholicism, Pugin became interested in Gothic architecture and was a leading exponent of the Gothic Revival style, working on the Houses of Parliament in London. When he died at age forty, the family practice was taken over by his two sons, Peter Paul and Edward Welby Pugin, by then partners in the famous London firm Pugin & Pugin.

Edward Woods

Born and educated in London, Edward Woods practised architecture before emigrating to Adelaide in 1860 and joining the firm of EW Wright, later Wright and Woods. In addition to the buildings listed above, the firm's designs included the Kent Town Methodist Church, St Lawrence's in North Adelaide, the Smyth Roman Catholic Chapel at West Terrace Cemetery and, with the Hamilton brothers, the Brougham Place Congregational Church in North Adelaide. In 1869, Woods established his own practice to oversee the first stage of St Peter's Cathedral and later, additions to St Francis Xavier Cathedral. In 1873 William McMinn joined Woods, who four years later became Architect in Chief for South Australia, responsible for many public buildings including the State Library, Museum and Art Gallery of SA on North Terrace and new Parliament House. Returning to private practice, in 1905 he invited former pupil, Walter Bagot, to join him and together they formed the firm of Woods Bagot.

Edmund Wright

Edmund William Wright was one of Australia's finest colonial architects. His family had French relatives and a summer home in an old chateau in France, which is where Edmund became familiar with his beloved French architecture. He trained in London as a civil engineer and architect and was the third of five brothers who arrived in Adelaide in 1850. Within a few short years he had become Mayor. With Edward Woods, he established an architectural practice, Wright and Woods, which designed some of Adelaide's grandest and most beautiful buildings. The few that remain include the Adelaide Town Hall, Parliament House, the General Post Office, Glenelg Town Hall and the building which now bears his name, Edmund Wright House. In 1886, he became the first Chairman of what was to become the South Australian Chapter of the Royal Australian Institute of Architects.

.98

INDEX

Adelaide Arcade, **28**, 92
Adelaide Casino, 50
Adelaide Central Market, 38
Adelaide Club, **8**, 10, 93
Adelaide Fruit and Produce Exchange, **38**, 58, 92
Adelaide Gaol, **84**, 94
Adelaide Railway Station, **50**
Adelaide Town Hall, **70**, 72, 93, 97
Advertiser, The, 76, 78
Albert Bridge, **86**
ANZ Bank, 46
Armoury, **16**, 60
Art Gallery of South Australia, **4**, 60, 97
Austral Hotel, **6**, 95
Austral Stores. See West's Coffee Palace
Australian Institute of Management, 74
Ayers House, **64**
Ayers, Harry, 66
Ayers, Henry, 64

Bagot, Walter, 12, 76, 78, **91**
Band Rotunda, **30**
Bank of South Australia, 46
Bethlehem Lutheran Church, **22**, 92
Bonython Hall, **76**, 91
Bonython, Sir Langdon, 36, 76
Bonython, Sir Lavington, 70
Botanic Chambers, **52**, 96
Botanic Gardens, 40, 52, 82
Botanic Hotel, 26, 52
Box, Mrs George, 10
Buffalo HMS, 32, 42, 48

Cawley, Dr Thomas, 10
Charlick, William, 38
City Market. See Adelaide Central Market
Colonial Store, **60**
Conrad, Albert, 58
Cotton, GW, 72

Cowell, Henry James, 38, **92**
Cumming, James, 22, 28, **92**

Daly, Sir Dominic, 70
Destitute Asylum Buildings, **18**
Destitute Asylum Chapel, **20**
Dimora, **66**, 95
Dunstan, Don, 46

East End Market. See Adelaide Fruit and Produce Exchange
Edmund Wright House, **46**, 97
Egan, Michael, **92**
Elder Park, 30
Elder School of Music, 14
Elder, Sir Thomas, 30
Electric Light Hotel. See Woodman's Inn
Evangelical Lutheran Church, **22**

Family Hotel. See Austral Hotel
Ferguson, Sir James, 42
Francis, George, 82
Fruit and Produce Exchange, 26

Garlick, Daniel, 56, 72, **93**
General Post Office, 70
Gosse, William, 64
Government House, 8, 34, **42**, 93, 94
Government Hut, 42
Governor Gawler, 42, 84
Governor Hindmarsh, 32, 42
Governor Jervois, 42
Grainger, John, 86
Grainger, Percy, 62, 86
Grant's Coffee Palace. See West's Coffee Palace

Hamilton, Edward Angus, 8, 42, **93**
Hampshire Hotel, **44**, 96
Hansom, Charles, 78, **93**

Hartley Building, **14**, 95
Hartley, John Anderson, 14
Hays, William Bennett, 16, 18, 34, **91**
Hindley Street Offices, **74**
Holy Trinity Church, 16, **32**
House of Assembly, 34, 36
Howard, Charles Beaumont, 32
Hughes, Sir Walter Watson, 80

Immigration Square, 32
Irish Row, 8

Justice Jeffcott, 48

Kingston, Charles Cameron, 56, 62
Kingston, George Strickland, 8, 42, 62, 64, 84, **94**

Lady Musgrave, 40
Lambeth, Richard, 48, 78, **94**
Lawson, George Gavin, 14, **95**
Legislative Council, 34, 36
Light, Colonel, 48, 56, 62, 78
Linger, Carl, 62
Lying-in Hospital, 18

Magistrates Court, **48**, 94
Malcolm Reid and Co, 6
Markets. *See* Adelaide Fruit and Produce Exchange
Maxwell, William J, 46
McDonnell, Sir Richard, 42
McLeay, John, 56
McMinn, William, 6, 12, 66, 72, 95
McMullen, Michael, 52, **96**
Melrose, Alexander, 4
Melrose, George, 4
Menz Biscuit Factory, 54
Menz, John, 54
Menz, Magdalena, 54

Migrant Resource Centre, 46
Migration Museum, 18, 68
Milne, Kenneth, 44, 74, **96**
Milne, Sir William, 12
Mitchell Building, **80**, 91, 92, 95
Mitchell, Dame Roma, 42
Mitchell, William, 80
Mortlock Library, 24
Moseley, Henry, 32
Mounted Police Barracks, **68**

National Trust museum, 64
New Colonial Store. *See* Colonial Store
Newmarket Hotel, **56**
North Lodge, **82**
North Terrace Townhouse, **12**

Old Parliament House, 16, 32, **34**, 36, 91, 94
Old Queens Theatre, 48
Oliphant, Sir Mark, 42

Palm House, **40**
Parliament House, 8, 34, **36**, 97
Pastor Kavel, 22
Paxton, William, 64
Prince Bismarck, 22
Producers Hotel. *See* Woodman's Inn
Pugin & Pugin, 78, **96**

Queen Adelaide Club, **10**
Queen's Chambers, **72**

Radford Auditorium, 60
Registry of Births, Deaths and Marriages, 46
Roman Catholic Chapel, **62**, 97
Rotunda March, 30
Runge, Gustav, 40

Schomburgk, Dr Richard, 40
Short, Bishop, 32

Smith, Edwin, 30
Smyth, Reverend John, 62
Solicitor-General, 48
South Australia Company, 6
South Australian Brewing Company, 26, 74
South Australian Mining Company, 64
South Australian Museum, 16, **24**, 68, 97
St Francis Xavier Cathedral, **78**, 91, 93, 94, 96, 97
St Stephen's Church, 22
Stag Hotel, 38
State Archives, 60
State Library and Museum, 4
State Library of South Australia, 18, 20
Strathmore Hotel, 50

Tandanya Aboriginal Cultural Centre, 26
Taylor, Lloyd, 36
Tennyson, Lord, 42
The Woodman. See Woodman's Inn
Thornber, Robert, 64
Torrens Lake, 30
Torrens River, 30, 86
Torrens, Robert, 86
Trinity Church. *See* Holy Trinity Church

Union Bank, 46
United Evangelical Lutheran Church, 22
University of Adelaide, 14, 68, 80

Vaughan, Richard, 38, 52
Victoria Square, 36, 48

Waterhouse, Arthur, 12
Webb, WA, 50
West's Coffee Palace, **58**
Woodman's Inn, **26**
Woods, Edward, 32, 36, 62, 70, 78, **97**
Wright, Edmund, 36, 46, 70, 72, **97**

ABOUT THE AUTHORS

Peter Fischer

With *Vintage Adelaide*, Peter Fischer has blended the latest in digital technology with a lifelong passion for architecture and photography.

While his early books, *Time Exposure* and *City in Focus* reflected this passion and made the most of the technology available at the time, the advent of digital photography has allowed Peter to continue developing his style, combining his technological skills with artistic endeavour. The result is a candid yet creative and inspired representation of some of Adelaide's most glorious buildings

Kay Hannaford Seamark

Kay first developed a love of Adelaide's history and its beautiful old buildings while living in the south-east corner of the city square mile and taking people on heritage tours in the 1980s.

Since returning recently from Sydney where she has lived since 1995, she now appreciates Adelaide's rich heritage with fresh eyes.